PART II –
TEENS

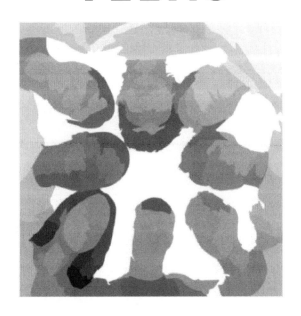

CONTENTS

INTRODUCTION

Why should you read this book?

- Your parent(s) cared enough about you to get and read this book

- It can get you more freedom in your teen years

- It is short and to the point

- It can help you be a better son or daughter

- It can make you a better friend

- It can make you a better person

- It can make your life easier

- It can make your life better

- You can learn helpful life skills

- It shows you care

- You might actually like it

LET'S GET TO IT!

Teens naturally want more freedom as they get older. Parents are often hesitant to give them the freedom they desire. This book helps parents and teens align to have a strong relationship that allows for more trust/freedom.

Your part of the book is much shorter than your parents :) Your parents will also want to talk to you about these topics in more detail. Please, do not roll your eyes and say, "I already know all of this!" Spend the time to hear them out and let them know what you know while keeping an open mind to learning from them.

CHAPTER 1:
TRUST

I t just makes sense that the more someone trusts you, the more freedom they will give you. Every parent and child dynamic differs, but this is true for all relationships. So how do you help your parents trust you? You talk to them, are honest and transparent with them, and hold yourself to a high standard. Let us look at each of these.

It is common for teens to come home and spend 95% of their time in their room, often avoiding family, especially parents. However, when someone knows and understands you, they feel more connected with you strengthening the relationship. The better the relationship, the stronger the trust. For example, let us say you are a parent with two teens, and one comes home from school and spends five to ten minutes telling you about his day. He shares what he had for lunch, a funny story from class, what practice was like, what his homework looks like – nothing earth-shattering but sharing little pieces of the day. The parent then asks a few questions or relates something from their day. The whole exchange is quick, but it is meaningful. The other teen goes to their room with a "hey" on the way through the house. As a parent, which teen would you feel more connected with? Obviously, the one that speaks more to you. It is a good idea to talk to your parents for many reasons, but establishing a strong relationship and trust is at the top of the list.

One tiny little lie can destroy so much trust. It just makes sense that if you lie about something small how can you be trusted with bigger things? A parent told me their teen lied about brushing their teeth. This parent really struggled to know what to believe after that one lie. You can tell 100 truths and one lie, but that one lie puts everything else into question. Parents virtually always find out the truth in the end; it is infinitely better if they hear it from you. Do not underestimate the need to be honest and trusted. It is incredibly powerful. Your integrity is so important! Telling one lie can lead to other lies and more problems. Strive to be honest in all you do.

It is also true that some parents can be hard to be honest with. They may react poorly or overreact to hearing something undesirable. It can be really helpful if you preface what you have to say with a warning. For example, if you did not brush your teeth saying something like, "I'll be honest with you, I did not, but I'll go do it now." If you must give unwelcome news, like flunking a math test or getting in trouble at school, saying something like, "Mom, Dad I need to tell you something and you're not going to like it." That little introduction lets them prepare to hear what you say, appreciate that you are being truthful, and have a more controlled response. (By the way, in the parent section, your parents also read this tip and are prepared to better receive what you have to tell them.) These tips work well with friends, teachers, and bosses as well. It does not mean they will not be upset, but it sets the stage for a much better discussion and resolution.

Do not be afraid to present your point of view. If you and your parents cannot agree on something and you feel strongly about it, then consider speaking up. First, do your research, have valuable information to support your point of view. Second, ask for a meeting letting them know what you want to discuss, so they also have time to prepare and consider their points as well. Third, be polite and respectful. If you act responsibly, you are more likely to be heard and your point of view considered. Maybe you cannot change your parents' mind, perhaps they are not willing to consider right now, but in the future, maybe you can compromise, or maybe your parents reconsider their point of view.

You will have what you i*ncest in yourself* at the end of your teen years. Your actions now affect your future. Your teachers will get paid whether you put forth your best effort or not and your parents will continue with their lives. You are the one that suffers if you are not being the best you can be and you are the one that excels if you have strived to do and be your best. Parents and teachers are in your life to help and guide you, but clearly, they cannot do the work for you. It must come from you! You owe it to yourself to set goals and be the best you can be. When your parents see you holding yourself to high standards and trying your best, they will give you more respect and trust. It is truly a win/win situation.

Below is an example of an exercise that can help you live your life more intentionally and help you strive for constant improvement. The thought is that once every month or two you honestly reflect on the key areas in your life. You consider what you are doing that is really working and strive to continue and build those good habits.

You also consider ways you can improve. Ideally you share your list with your parent(s) and invite their input. They may see things you are not aware of and help you grow or fine tune your list. When they know your goals and struggles, they will be better prepared to support you and encourage you. It will help your parent(s) understand you and trust you more. Your parent(s) are encouraged to make their own list to share with you. This exercise invites giving and receiving feedback, which is a skill you are going to need lifelong. Give this a try! It will likely be awkward in the beginning but should grow into a version you can really benefit from. Personalize the exercise to meet your needs best and make self-reflection and betterment a part of your lifelong habits. You really have nothing to lose and so much to gain.

SAMPLE TEEN SELF-REFLECTION EXERCISE

Area	What I am doing well	Where I can improve
School	- Turning in assignments	- Talking to teachers and asking for help
	- Organized	- Attending tutorials
	- Having the correct supplies	- Making up work when I miss
	- Not procrastinating on projects	- Being on time
Home	- In by curfew	- Cleaning up after myself
	- Keeping room orderly	- Communicating plans/schedule/needs
	- Doing assigned chores	- Quality time with parents
	- Spending quality time with siblings	- Getting up and out of bed on my own with the alarm
		- Not talking back
Sports	- Encouraging teammate	- Better stretching
	- Putting in the hard work and effort	- Better hydration
Personal	- Eating three healthy meals a day	- Limiting electronic time (social media, videos, texting, etc.)
	- Getting daily aerobic exercise	- Get a goal of eight hours of sleep a night
	- Managing stress with constructive techniques	- Limit snacking
	- Good skin care and hygiene	- Control anger better
Social	- Trying new experiences	- Be a better listener
	- Helpful to friends/kind	- Follow through on my promises
Faith	- Making strong moral choices	- Daily prayer
		- Being more grateful
Job		- Fill out applications and get one

CHAPTER 15:
FRIENDSHIPS

Remember when it comes to friends that it is better to have a few quality friends than a large quantity of "friends." Your friends should like you for you, you should not have to change to be liked. Friends should build you up by being supportive and encouraging. You will likely do what your friends do, so make sure your friends are making good choices and align with your beliefs and goals for yourself. It is natural to want to be liked, just make sure you are liked for the right reasons. Hold yourself to a high standard in all areas, including friendships Surround yourself with those who will better your life, push you to succeed, and be there in tough times. Do not be afraid to realign friend groups if your friends are not making strong choices, not being supportive, or pushing you to do something you are not comfortable with.

Do not underestimate the power of a smile or a kind word. Try to meet as many students as possible in each of your classes. You never know where you might find a shared interest that can spark a new friendship. One of my sons met an incredible friend while checking his car app. The two started talking and realized they shared a love of cars. That chance encounter grew into a really supportive and fun friendship.

CHAPTER 16

MENTAL HEALTH

Teen years are not easy. They come with a lot of stress. Stress can lead to anxiety and anxiety to depression. If you are anxious or depressed it is not your fault and you are certainly not alone, but please reach out for help. We are all better and stronger when we get the help we need, and you can learn skills that will last you a lifetime.

As you get older you take on more responsibility and that increases stress. Find effective ways for handling your stress. There is not one right way to cope with stress–find what works for you. Here are a few suggestions:

- Take three deep breaths – breathe in slowly, hold, and exhale

- Exercise

- Talk it out with friends, parents, or another trusted adult

- Journal

- Listen to music or play music

- A warm bath or shower

- Draw or another artistic outlet

- Read a book

- Pray

When your stress level is out of control it can affect every area of your life. Sleep might become hard or interrupted. You may eat to try and cope with stress or stop eating due to stress. Grades, friendships, sports or other activities can all suffer. Be proactive and reach out for help from your parents, your pediatrician, schoolteacher, school counselor, or another trusted adult. The sooner you get help the sooner you get back to your best self!

CHAPTER 17:
DRUGS

I t just takes one time trying a drug to be addicted for life or dead. Do not try them-not even once! You cannot be sure what is in it or how your body will react. It is not worth the risk. I have seen amazing kids have their lives forever changed from a one-time drug use. Plan how to say NO and walk away. Keep all your dreams on track. Be cautious of everything. Do not take candy, supplements, or over-the-counter pills unless you are 100% certain where it came from. Friends would not intentionally give you something harmful, but if you did not see them buy the item at a reputable store, be safe and do not take it. It is simply not worth the risk of it being tainted.

If you are using drugs, ask for help today! The longer you use any drug the harder it will be to stop and to get your life back on track. You will have a much greater chance of lifelong addiction and advancing to even stronger and more dangerous drugs. You have so much to lose! Sure, your parents will be upset and disappointed, but you need their help, and they deserve your honesty. You can get through this and be better together. If you truly feel you cannot start by asking your parents for help, ask another trusted adult. The important thing is to get help and not to wait. **Take this step towards getting your life back today.**

CHAPTER 18:
SEX

Contrary to widespread belief, not everyone is having sex. Approximately 30% – 35% of teenagers choose to be sexually active and the other 65-70% choose to wait. If you decide to be sexually active, educate yourself first. You can get pregnant and a sexually transmitted disease the very first time. If you are considering being sexually active, make sure you are emotionally ready, choose for yourself while not feeling pressured, and prepare yourself in advance. Ideally, talk to your parents beforehand.

CHAPTER 19

SOCIAL MEDIA

Social media can be useful. It can let you be creative, stay informed, and further friendships. However, it can easily and quickly become a negative. It must be used responsibly. That means for limited periods and in a positive manner. You do not want to lose valuable sleep or homework time to social media. Always remember that what is posted rarely reflects the whole picture—meaning photoshop, filters and no one's life is perfect.

CHAPTER 20:
SELF-CARE

The habits you start now will likely be what you continue for the rest of your life. If you picture yourself as fit and healthy at forty, fifty, or sixty, start taking good care of yourself today. Strive to eat healthily. This means not overeating, avoiding emotional eating, or eating out of boredom, and maintaining a healthy diet. Healthy eating looks like consuming lots of vegetables, fruits, and proteins while minimizing carbohydrates, fats, and sugars. One hour of activity is recommended daily. Be active and creative in the ways you get your exercise. Teens need eight to ten hours of sleep per night. Prioritize your sleep. We are all better when we are rested! (More info on healthy sleep habits is available in Chapter 5 of the parent section under the subtitle of Sleep.)

CHAPTER 21:
FAMILY

As a teen, your friends, school, and activities are naturally a huge part of your world. It can be easy to ignore or take your family for granted, but family *is* important. It is OK not to have a traditional family and no one has a perfect family. Make an effort to connect with parents, siblings, grandparents, aunts, uncles, and cousins (or depending on your situation, others in your life that can fill those roles). Let the support of your family help guide you and strengthen you. Family bonds often know you the best, are stronger, and last well beyond the teen years.

CHAPTER 22:
FAITH

For many, faith is their go-to for answers and guidance, especially in challenging times. It is normal and healthy for you to question faith. Your thoughts and ideas may closely complement the beliefs of your family, or you might find your thoughts and ideas of faith contrasting with your family. Talk to your family about what they believe in and why. Ask questions and figure out what role faith can play in your life. If you are not comfortable talking to your family about faith, look for other resources for reliable information. Possible sources might be friends, mentors, religious leaders, or vetted online information sites. Some of the happiest teens I meet are strong in their faith. Faith can be your best resource and strength for your teen years and the rest of your life.

CHAPTER 23:
CONCLUSION

Your teen years and beyond are a time of figuring out who you are, what you are about, where you fit in, how you want to represent yourself, what standards you will set for yourself and hold yourself accountable to, and what you want for yourself. Teen years are about who you are becoming. You want to be smart, intentional, and purposeful in developing yourself. It is not easy, but it is your chance to live your best life. Look to those you admire as an example, guide and mentor. Do not be afraid to ask questions and ask for help.

Your efforts will not be perfect. You will make mistakes. This is normal and can be a valuable way to learn and become stronger. No one is perfect. Make things right and move forward. Often, we learn more from our mistakes than our successes.

IN CLOSING:

You do not get to pick your life or circumstances, but you can push yourself to be your absolute best. You can choose to work hard and hold yourself to high standards. You can choose to constantly work at bettering yourself.

If you do – you benefit.

If you do not – you lose.

It is really in your hands. No one else can make you a good person, make you successful, or make your dreams a reality. Others may help, support, or encourage you, but your life is yours to live. My hope is that you make the very most of it!

CHAPTER 24:
TEEN REFLECTION QUESTIONS

1. What can I do to be a better son or daughter?

2. What can I do to be a better friend?

3. What can I do to be a better student?

4. How can I strengthen my communication skills?

5. What two areas of self-care do I need to focus on most?

6. How can I ask for help or support in these areas?

7. Who do I admire and why?

8. How can I hold myself to a higher standard?

9. Who can help make me accountable?

10. What are three goals I want to accomplish in the next year?

11. What are three goals I want to accomplish in the next five years?

BIBLIOGRAPHY

"American Heart Association Recommendations for Physical Activity in Adults and Kids." *Www.Heart.Org*, 28 July 2022, www.heart.org/en/healthy-living/fitness/fitness-basics/aha-recs-for-physical-activity-in-adults.

Chapman, Gary. "Learn More about Yourself." *Learn More About Yourself*, 5lovelanguages.com/quizzes/.

"Get the Facts about Underage Drinking." *National Institute on Alcohol Abuse and Alcoholism*, U.S. Department of Health and Human Services, www.niaaa.nih.gov/publications/brochures-and-fact-sheets/underage-drinking.

Hyder, Eileen, and Lucinda Becker. "How to make your social media communication inclusive." *Inclusive Communication*, 2022, https://doi.org/10.4135/9781071901205.

New, Michael J. *The Corner: New CDC Data Shows Continued Decline in Teen Sexual Activity*. Owlkids Books, 2023.

Suni, Eric, and Alex Dimitriu. *National Sleep Foundation Pamphlets*. National Sleep Foundation.

"Tween and Teen Health Tween and Teen Health." *Mayo Clinic*, Mayo Foundation for Medical Education and Research, 23 Aug. 2023, www.mayoclinic.org/healthy-lifestyle/tween-and-teen-health/basics/tween-and-teen-health/hlv-20049436.

"Underage Drinking." *Centers for Disease Control and Prevention*, Centers for Disease Control and Prevention, 26 Oct. 2022, www.cdc.gov/alcohol/fact-sheets/underage-drinking.htm.

ABOUT THE AUTHOR

D r. Julie Messner is passionate about helping kids of all ages while supporting and encouraging parents and caregivers. She is a mom of four very wonderful and quite different children. Two have recently graduated from the teen years, the third is about to exit teen years and the fourth is just getting started. Her kiddos have taught her so much and helped her grow as a mother, pediatrician, and person.

She also has an over fifteen-year relationship with an orphanage in Honduras. She loves these children as her own. Over the years, she has seen babies and toddlers grow into teens and young adults who need to find their place in a challenging world. She strives to educate and prepare these fragile kiddos for life outside the orphanage.

In addition, Dr. Messner enjoys educating, advising, and supporting her patients within her pediatric practice. She has learned so much from listening to her teen patients through the years and hearing of their struggles and concerns. She cherishes the trust they place in her to guide them. In her over twenty-five years of practice, she has delighted in helping teens and parents unite to form a greater understanding and support of one another. She wants each of her patients to live their absolute best lives.

It is from these passions and experiences that Dr. Messner decided to author this book and share her experiences with the sincere hope of strengthening more families and making the teen years much more rewarding and successful for both parents and teens.

A part of the proceeds from this book will go to fund the orphanage that Dr. Messner supports.

THRIVING
THE
TEEN
YEARS

Beyond Surviving

JULIE MESSNER

Edited by Patricia Ogilvie, Pro Risk Enterprises Ltd.

ISBN: 979-8-35092-950-8
eBook ISBN: 979-8-35092-951-5

ABOUT THE AUTHOR

D r. Julie Messner is passionate about helping kids of all ages while supporting and encouraging parents and caregivers. She is a mom of four very wonderful and quite different children. Two have recently graduated from the teen years, the third is about to exit teen years and the fourth is just getting started. Her kiddos have taught her so much and helped her grow as a mother, pediatrician, and person.

She also has an over fifteen-year relationship with an orphanage in Honduras. She loves these children as her own. Over the years, she has seen babies and toddlers grow into teens and young adults who need to find their place in a challenging world. She strives to educate and prepare these fragile kiddos for life outside the orphanage.

In addition, Dr. Messner enjoys educating, advising, and supporting her patients within her pediatric practice. She has learned so much from listening to her teen patients through the years and hearing of their struggles and concerns. She cherishes the trust they place in her to guide them. In her over twenty-five years of practice, she has delighted in helping teens and parents unite to form a greater understanding and support of one another. She wants each of her patients to live their absolute best lives.

It is from these passions and experiences that Dr. Messner decided to author this book and share her experiences with the sincere hope of strengthening more families and making the teen years much more rewarding and successful for both parents and teens.

A part of the proceeds from this book will go to fund the orphanage that Dr. Messner supports.

DEDICATION

I am indebted to many who have blessed my life:

I am immensely grateful to my incredible parents who have shown me unconditional love and given me such a solid foundation.

My four children have made my life so complete and wonderful while teaching me so much. I love all of you more than you will ever know and am so thankful you call me Mom.

Dan, your love and encouragement give me the confidence to be more.

I have learned from many colleagues through the years and owe them my sincere gratitude.

I so appreciate all the patients and their families who have trusted me with their care.

Many family members and friends have adamantly supported me and my children through the most difficult times and celebrated with us in the joyful times. Thank you for being with us!

CONTENTS

PART I –
PARENTS

INTRODUCTION

Parenting a teen can be exhausting and challenging, but it can also be one of the most meaningful, impactful, and rewarding things you ever do. The reward of intentional, loving, and supportive teen parenting is immense, with an enormous impact on each family, community, and future generations.

When I was about three years old, I sucked my thumb. My Mother desperately wanted me to stop this habit. She tried all the recommendations from our doctor, neighbors, and grandparents. Nothing worked. She was desperate! Finally, she went against all recommendations and bribed me. She offered to get me anything I wanted if I would stop sucking my thumb. I requested a real working stethoscope. My mother bought the best stethoscope she could find, and I stopped sucking my thumb. Parenting often involves knowing your child, creativity, and thinking outside the box.

If all teens were the same, there would be one teen manual for every parent to read and reference. Each parent would know precisely what to do and what not to do at what age and stage of development. Raising teens would be easy! Unfortunately, no such manual will ever exist as every teen is different, and the world they are growing up in is constantly changing. There are, however, several concepts, ideas, and suggestions that are uniformly helpful.

The mission of this book is to create strong parent and teen bonds, making parenting a teen less stressful, more enjoyable, successful, and impactful. My sincere hope is for you to leave the teen years with a young adult and parent connection that is full of mutual respect and a strong relationship for all the years to follow. You will notice that the chapters in this book are short. My approach is direct, practical, and to the point. I hope being concise makes reading more feasible for many parents. Applying just a few of the thoughts and ideas from this book to your teen relationship can be a game changer for you and your child.

Truth without relationship leads to rejection. Rules without relationship lead to rebellion. Discipline without relationship leads to bitterness, anger, and resentment. To effectively lead and develop someone you have to have a relationship with them. It is through relationships that you can shape people to be their best.

– Josh McDowell

This quote exemplifies the importance of forming a strong relationship with your child. So, as of today, you must start where you are, as we cannot change the past.

- If your relationship is already good, look for ways to make it even better.

- If your relationship is poor, start fresh today to build a better one.

- If your relationship is great, continue building upon what you have.

Even the best relationships are complicated and ever-changing. As you read this book, see what ideas might work for you, and do not be afraid to seek professional counseling and help if needed. Change does not happen overnight, but each positive encounter builds a better relationship. Sometimes something as seemingly minor as changing perspective can lead to huge gains. Look for small victories and celebrate them. Parents want to be successful, but many need help knowing where to start or feel like their relationship with their teen is slipping away. Let us get reading and find ways to shape and change the future for you and your teen!

CHAPTER 1:
RELATIONSHIP

I t is said that with relationships, you get what you put into them. With a teen relationship, it might feel like you, as the parent, are the only one putting much into the relationship. In some ways, this is expected. As teens figure out growing independence and responsibilities, they may take their parents for granted. They are unlikely to fully realize the importance of relationships, especially with their parents, and unlikely to know much about being in a relationship. Their energies may be pulled in many directions, and they may not understand that they need their parents. Some may feel they already have all the answers, and some may be struggling but do not know how to ask for help. They need their parents to take the lead and meet them where they are.

The parent must put in the effort even when the teen does not meet it. Whether they admit it or not, they need you. The parent is called to lead and not give up. You must be the constant in your teen's life, dig in, and try even harder when times get rough. Parenting is not for the selfish or faint of heart. It can be challenging work and doing what your teen needs you to do, even when you do not feel like it, twenty-four hours a day, seven days a week! Just keep showing up and being present. Many successful adults have credited one or both parents for being there for them and not giving up on them during their difficult teen years. You matter so much to your teen, even if they do not fully realize your impact at this point in their life. Do not underestimate the effect of being present in your child's life.

Tell your teen how much you love them and want to be there for them through the good and the hard. Let them know you are committed to being there for them. Let them know how much they mean to you and that there is nothing they can do to destroy that love. You may not always like them or what they do, but you always love them. You may disagree with them on small and even large matters, but you always love them. You may not trust them, but you will always love them. You might be super frustrated with them, but you love them! Remind them of this often. Be the constant in their ever-changing world! It will give them confidence. It will help them succeed.

Treating others how you want to be treated is great advice for everyone, including teens. Treat your teen with respect. Be honest with your teen. Honor your word with your teen. Apologize when you mess up and own your mistakes. You are the role model for your child. It is unlikely your teen will be honest with you if they know you are not being honest with them. In small and large matters, being trustworthy is crucial. If you want your teen to treat you respectfully, treat them respectfully even when they fall short. When you role model respectful behavior, it will more likely be returned to you in time. Show them how to agree to disagree. You can respect their opinion even if you do not share that opinion. If you are late picking them up, apologize. Yes, you may have a particularly good reason for being late, and they are fortunate it was only ten minutes, but acknowledge that you kept them waiting. It shows you care and value being on time.

Consider sitting down with your teen and asking for their feedback. What do you do that they like? What would they want you to add? What would they change? What is the best way and time to talk to them? Is there anything interfering with the relationship? How can you pray for them? Open the lines of communication and let them know you value their feedback.

I will admit the first time I did this with my son, he did not list many things that I did that he liked, and he had a lengthy list of dislikes. It turns out it really annoyed him when I did not fully close the bedroom door when I left his room. Fortunately, I took his feedback gracefully, and a little later in the day, he added more to his positive list. It really impacted him that I cared about and received his opinions. It opened a new line of communication. The door closing seemed insignificant to me, but was an easy change once I knew it was important to him. You might not always be able to honor their feedback, but you can receive it and consider it.

Schedule intentional family time with respect to everyone's schedule and make it required. Eating dinner together as a family may not be possible every night but should be part of the routine as often as possible. If not dinner, consider Sunday brunch or evening snacks that can be made together with a bit of fun, like S'mores or ice cream sundaes. Be creative and try joint meals frequently along with other family activities. Go for a walk, volunteer together, play cards or board games, shoot hoops, cook together, watch a movie, etc. Let simple activities become fun family traditions.

When my oldest was four, he loved trains. I purchased a gingerbread train set, and he, his two-year-old brother and I had such a great time assembling and decorating the train. We have done a gingerbread activity every year for twenty years now. Since they are older and there are four of them, it often looks like teams competing in decorating gingerbread houses. It is something we all look forward to each year. Even though they do not trick-or-treat anymore, we still carve or paint pumpkins in the fall. We dye Easter eggs in the spring. Seeing their creativity is fun, and we make memories and form stronger bonds doing it together. It just takes a little planning ahead to get everyone together. Be open to spontaneous unplanned fun as well.

The 5 Love Languages by Gary Chapman can be a great resource (see 5lovelanguages.com). One night I had all my kiddos take the love language quiz that revealed how they like to receive affection. Naturally, there were different answers for all four of my children. Knowing how they scored explained why some things I did for them were well received and appreciated while others seemed less valued. It helped me understand how to focus my energies to connect with them better. For example, one child scored high in physical touch. Simple acts like greeting them with a hug or squeezing their arm as I walked by reached them more than lots of praising words. Knowing some scored high in quality time made me plan more one-on-one time with them than group activities. Another liked words of affirmation so lunch box notes were added. We enjoyed taking the quiz together and hearing each other's results. It became an even more fun night when we took other quizzes like which Disney princess are you and What is your mental age? We all laughed a lot and learned more about each other.

CHAPTER 2:
RESIST COMPARING

I t is extremely easy to compare your teen to their siblings, friends, classmates, what you were like at their age, what you see on social media, etc. Nothing positive will come out of these comparisons! Each child is unique and must find their way.

I grew up with an identical twin sister. Being a twin was great in many ways but from the earliest age we were compared. It is just natural to see one is bigger, talks more, smiles more, or is more active. There is a wide range of normal and differences are usually just that—different ways of being or doing something. In my teen years, frequent comparison made me feel competitive, and not always in positive ways. I had to learn over time to celebrate our differences and let each of us grow into the best version of ourselves.

Some kids mature faster than others. A few may be very responsible and organized from an early age while others may take years to reach that same level. I have had many mothers tell me that they never dreamed their son would be a successful college student. They relayed getting through high school was an incredibly difficult struggle, and they just knew their child would not make it through college. Then slowly they start to see the maturity and about four years later they are graduating with honors much to the delight and surprise of their parents. These kiddos just needed support till they matured. They were slower than their peers but found their way. Strive to meet and embrace your teen where they are now and support them as the unique individual they are.

As a parent, it can be difficult to find the balance between coddling your child or helicopter parenting vs. too much independence too soon. Knowing how much support vs. independence they need and when can be challenging. The teen years are about them learning to let go and become independent while having the safety net of parents. They go from clinging to your leg and falling asleep in your arms to running out the door with car keys in their hands. It is a considerable change in a relatively brief period for both the parent and the child.

One idea I have shared frequently over the years has had a lot of success in helping both the teen and the parent. The idea is to live intentionally trying to be the best you. By doing this exercise with your teen, you can gain valuable insight into their thoughts and world. It can be a resource for you to celebrate what they are doing well and help them grow in areas of struggle. It can help you know them better and appreciate them for who they are vs. comparing them to other standards. It works best when both the parent and the child participate together in this exercise. It works like this:

EXERCISE FOR INTENTIONAL LIVING

Pick a date once every month or two to do a self-review. The parent and the teen make lists of what they feel they are doing well and areas they would like to improve. Ideally, these are detailed lists that address many areas of life. The idea is to continue growing the areas you excel in and work on the areas of weakness. Once the parent and child have composed their lists, they review them with each other and are open to what each other sees in them. You grow your list together and support each other as you better understand what each person is working toward. This teaches and reinforces working to be the best version of yourself, being receptive to feedback, and giving constructive and balanced feedback. It could look something like this:

SAMPLE TEEN VERSION

Area	What I am doing well	Where I can improve
School	- Turning in assignments	- Talking to teachers and asking for help
	- Organized	- Attending tutorials
	- Having the correct supplies	- Making up work when I miss
	- Not procrastinating on projects	- Being on time
Home	- In by curfew	- Cleaning up after myself
	- Keeping room orderly	- Communicating plans/schedule/needs
	- Doing assigned chores	- Quality time with parents
	- Spending quality time with siblings	- Getting up and out of bed on my own with the alarm
		- Not talking back
Sports	- Encouraging teammate	- Better stretching
	- Putting in the hard work and effort	- Better hydration
Personal	- Eating three healthy meals a day	- Limiting electronic time (social media, videos, texting, etc.)
	- Getting daily aerobic exercise	- Get a goal of eight hours of sleep a night
	- Managing stress with constructive techniques	- Limit snacking
	- Good skin care and hygiene	- Control anger better
Social	- Trying new experiences	- Be a better listener
	- Helpful to friends/kind	- Follow through on my promises
Faith	- Making strong moral choices	- Daily prayer
		- Being more grateful
Job		- Fill out applications and get one

SAMPLE PARENT VERSION

Area	What I am doing well	Where I can improve
Home	- Bills paid on time	- Better quality healthier meals
	- Planning quality family times	- Better communication – especially with schedule changes
	- Keeping home clean and organized	- Clean up yard
	- Managing calendar and activities	- Take down Christmas decorations
Work	- Leaving work finished at office and not bringing it home	- Advance my education
	- Helpful/friendly coworker	- Be on time
	- Well respected and trusted	- Organize my workspace/office
Personal	- Trustworthy and reliable	- Get more sleep
	- Almost daily walks/exercise	- Eat healthy
	- Staying calm in anxiety-provoking situations	- Self-care
	- Strong communicator	- Not texting and driving
Faith	- In scripture daily	- Share faith with my family/friends
	- Strong prayer life	- Attend church services more regularly
Social	- Responding timely to texts	- Be more spontaneous
	- Following up on friends in need	- Go welcome new neighbors
	- Planning activities to be with others (dinner with friends)	- Be better at apologizing and admitting when I am wrong
		- Be more demonstrative in my love of others

These lists are to start ideas flowing and can be customized to each person with more areas added and more details. You can refine the lists together with each other's feedback. The more specific and detailed the better! What your teen may see as a weakness you might see as a positive. Your teen may be struggling with how to fix a weakness, and you might be able to share a comparable situation in your life and how you handled it to spark ideas for them. If you know, for example, they need help with good hydration during sports, you can get them a bigger water bottle or pick them up with a cold drink waiting in the car. It is a minor change that helps them, and without a chance to sit down and discuss, you might not have known about that struggle. If they know you want to go to welcome the new neighbors, they might have time to bake cookies, and you can take them over together. Sharing goals allows for a better understanding of one another and intentionally directed support of one another. This process allows for self-awareness and intentional living. It is way too easy to wake up each day, make it through the day, and repeat the next day. This pushes you to be better.

Taking a little time each month or two to reflect on what is going well and needs to be continued and looking for areas to improve can be a powerful tool for you and your child lifelong. It is also powerful for both parent and child to be involved in the process together. It shows your teen that you are still learning and growing as an adult and striving to be your best. Doing this exercise with your teen shows you are committed to being the best version of yourself just as you hope and expect them to be the best version of themselves. By doing it together, you are not sending the message that the teen is the only one who needs to improve. You are not asking them to do something that you are not willing to do yourself. Learning to give and receive constructive feedback is vital at every age.

The first few times might be a little awkward, but like with most things, it should get easier over time. Try to make this time fun. You could go out for coffee, ice cream, or a meal to discuss the list. Commit to this monthly or bimonthly by marking it on the calendar and honor the date. If it must be missed, reschedule ASAP. Set the expectation that no one interrupts the other. Both parties are actively listening and thoughtfully responding. If emotions start to run high suggest a small break and then resume. If your faith leads you, start and end each session with a prayer. The discussion can be for just two or a family event. Young children might need help to grasp the concept fully and could be more of a distraction. Twelve years of age in general is a good starting age, but again every child varies in maturity. It should be taken seriously but leave room for laughter and lightheartedness as well.

The hope is this exercise will help you know your teen better so that you understand what is important to them, where their gifts and talents lie, and where they struggle. By better understanding them you appreciate them as the individual they are and are less tempted to compare them to others. An added benefit is that they get to appreciate you as well. Understanding each other is key. It leads to better conversations, being more supportive and less comparing.

CHAPTER 3:
COMMUNICATION

Words are so powerful! A simple compliment can bring a smile and turn the day around while harsh words can be devastating and never unsaid. There is an analogy of mean words being like nails driven into a wooden board. You can pull the nail out, but the hole in the board remains forever.

Communication is a vital part of any relationship, but especially with teens. It is just natural that the more your teen talks to you, the more you will know about them and trust them. It is also natural that they start talking to their friends more and less to you. It is possible that they see you as unapproachable, hard to talk to, or out of touch. It is possible that most of what they hear from you is negative and they start to block you out. However, communication has never been more vital or needed.

The first step to communicating is listening. All too often, while someone is talking, we are preparing our response and not really hearing them, or worse we jump in and start talking over them. We can assume we know what they are going to say or that we know better. As the adult in this relationship the parent needs to model effective communication skills. This means listening carefully and thoughtfully, processing what you heard, responding only after listening. In a disagreement it is helpful to restate what you heard to clarify that you are understanding before you reply. This process is not natural. It is practiced and learned, but it is a skill you want for both you and your teen.

Be approachable! When your teen attempts to talk to you, give them your full undivided attention. This sounds simple but enter the real world—as they start to talk while you are folding laundry, making dinner, unloading the dishwasher, answering a text, attending another child, exhausted, or running out the door (or some combination of that list). It can be hard to STOP, but your teen needs to know you are fully listening. That you value what they want to tell you. They are likely to tell you more and talk to you repeatedly if they feel heard and not like they are interrupting you. If you truly cannot listen at that moment, try saying something like, "I really want to hear this, can you give me 5 minutes to wrap up and be more present?"

Ask your teen to let you know when they are about to tell you something you might not like. A trick as simple as saying, "Hey Mom and Dad, I need to tell you something, and you're not going to like it." can be huge. When a parent hears those words, it helps them mentally prepare for what they are about to hear. It lets them know their child is being honest with them and prevents overreacting which makes the teen want to hide need-to-know information in the future.

If your teen comes up to you after a hectic workday while sorting mail full of bills and says, "I bombed the math test" you might not be in the best place to process that new piece of information without overreacting. In fact, you might say something like, "WHAT! I knew you were not studying hard enough for that test. I told you to study more!" or something even worse than those words. While you might be right about their study habits, that reaction does not make your teen want to tell you similar information in the future.

Hopefully, if your teen had prepared you by saying, "I need to give you some bad news.," then you would have taken a deep breath before responding and say something more along the lines of, "What went wrong?" Then they could tell you that theirs was one of the higher grades for the test and the teacher has decided to re-teach the test subjects and offer a new test next week.

Alternatively, they could say you were right, I needed to plan better for that test. I ran out of study time the night before and I was not well prepared. An open constructive conversation about better time management and study habits could follow. Maybe they are struggling and need a tutor or to go to tutorials. Whatever the case, the second response invites a much better interaction, problem solving and invites the likelihood of them telling you more about their grades in the future then an impulsive reaction which made them feel bad, did not have a productive discussion, and guarantees they will not want to tell you about future grades.

Do not be afraid to ask for a do-over. Show your teen that you are human and make mistakes. If you realize your part of a discussion was reactionary, judgmental, emotional or that you could just do better, apologize for how the first conversation went and ask to try again. There is a good chance the second time around will go much better.

Alternatively, if you are in a discussion that gets off track, consider signaling a time-out to take a deep breath, collect your thoughts and start anew in a more productive way mid-conversation. You and your teen will both benefit. By doing either the do-over or time-out, you have shown your teen you are trying and care. They have also learned about better communication and might need a do-over or time-out with you or a friend in the future.

Parents and teens can have remarkably busy lives with little time for conversation. You may only see them for a few minutes as they come and go. It is easy to fall into a habit of greeting them with things like, "Put away your clothes," "I told you to clean your room," or "Have you done your homework?" It is essential to make those quick moments count. Teens need to hear positive reinforcement along with the needed reminders.

Check your interactions to ensure you compliment and reinforce the good behaviors while correcting the negative. No one likes being around someone who is negative toward them much of the time and parents can feel they have such little time with their teen that they have to get in all the corrections while forgetting to add praise. That usually leads to the teen blocking out the parent. Seek out times to just offer positive words of encouragement. A simple "Thanks for taking out the trash.," "I really like that outfit." or "I like your dedication to your team." can lift them up and show you notice them.

Within reason, do not be afraid to tell your teen about your stresses. You certainly do not want to burden them with all your grown-up worries but at the same time they are likely to notice if you are not yourself and a simple explanation can prove helpful. Something like, "I have a huge project coming due at work so I may seem distracted. If you can help me out a bit more and give me some extra grace, I would sure appreciate it." or "Your Grandmother being ill is really weighing heavy on my mind, I'm feeling overwhelmed right now with decisions." Clearly you do not want to be a parent that dumps all their worries and concerns on their child, but it is helpful to let them know the basics about what is causing you extra stress when appropriate. By communicating your concerns, you allow your teen to try and understand and even support you. They can benefit from seeing you handle your stresses and hopefully, it encourages them to share their struggles with you.

It is not unusual for teens to be interested in something that parents really do not care much about and quite frankly are tired of hearing about. It is worth it to dig deep, learn about their interests, and share their enthusiasm. Meeting them where they are for this moment in time creates a needed bond. Sometimes, you must work with what they give you, even if it is not of your choosing. For example, one of mine loves video games. I really do not! I do, however, have a much better understanding of video games after entering his world and learning more. I understand why they are important to him and how he uses some of his video game connections and skills in other areas of his life. I can appreciate what he sees in them, even if they are not for me. Our relationship is undoubtedly strengthened by his willingness to share with me and my desire to learn.

CHAPTER 4:
FAMILY AND SUPPORT

Family can look traditional or nontraditional. There is not one right way to be a family. If you are blessed to have many close relatives to pour into and support your child, then take advantage of that incredible resource. Invite them to dinners, holidays, recitals, sports, etc. The more people that love and care about your children the better. Not all family members have to be biological relatives. Others can be used to fill those roles. Growing up my nieces had immediate family members that loved and cared for them, but they also found grandparents in Ron and Mary across the street. This sweet couple with grown children loved and supported the girls like the absolute best of grandparents, celebrating all their accomplishments and encouraging them. They provided lots of rides, dinners, hugs, and encouragement while being strong role models. A lifelong bond was formed for the benefit of all.

It is quite possible that at some point in their lives, your teen will relate better to someone besides you. Looking for trusted adults at church, work, school, in the neighborhood, and among your friends to mentor your child can be a blessing for all. Chances are this additional resource for your teen is validating what you have already told them, but they hear it differently or louder coming from someone who is not their parent. Do not be afraid to ask a trusted acquaintance to take your child to dinner, coffee, a game, etc. Create opportunities for them to bond with other role models. Fill their lives with solid examples to mentor them. Finding support from others can be especially important for single parents. Many single parents put unnecessary pressure on themselves to do it all. We are better and stronger when we allow for help. You can do it all but at the price of increased stress, self-exhaustion, and denying your teen the chance to bond with another. Consider looking into community mentoring programs like Big Brothers or Big Sisters. Be open to help. You never know who might positively impact your child's life.

CHAPTER 5:
WHAT EVERY PARENT NEEDS TO KNOW

Our teens are growing up in an ever-changing world. There are discussions that must be had and many of them repeated frequently and grown over time. Ideally, discussing these topics with your teen is not lecture style but an open, honest, informative exchange. Anytime you can personalize the discussion with examples from your own life it makes it more meaningful, relatable, and relevant. If you do not have a personal example, then one from this book, a friend, or the headlines can help your teen understand why it is so important to you that the two of you have this discussion. You have a lot of information you need them to know, but not all at once. Too much information can be overwhelming. The best discussions start small and grow as they are revisited. You must meet your teen at their current knowledge level. Let them know you are always available for questions. Let them know you will be honest with them and give them the best knowledge and advice you have to offer. Also, let them know you are willing to learn with them. These next topic discussions aim to help you have ideas, information and starting points to start your own conversations about these key areas in your child's life.

FRIENDSHIPS

To many teens, their friends are THEIR EVERYTHING. They are looking to be liked and accepted. Their friend's opinion matters as much if not more than their parent's opinion. Friends can be a huge blessing if they have strong, supportive friends whose values align with your child's values. This is the overall goal, but it rarely happens without some effort. As a parent you want to get to know your child's friends and ideally their parents as well. I tell my own children and patients that they may have close friends who begin to gravitate toward habits not in their best interest. If they continue to hang around friends making poor choices, it is often just a matter of time before your teen makes similar choices. Even the strongest teen can be worn down in a moment of weakness or peer pressure. I support being kind to that friend but distancing themself from them. My hope is that the friend will realize that they are making a poor choice over time and stop the harmful habit and the friendship can resume in a healthy way. For example, a friend decides to start vaping. Your teen does not choose to vape. They stay kind to their vaping friend, but do not hang out with them. After a few months of vaping the teen realizes choosing to vape was stupid and harming their health. They stop for good. Now, hopefully the relationship can resume in a healthy way. Teens owe it to themself to be surrounded by quality friends that build them up. I remind them that with friends it is truly quality over quantity. Having one or two close and trusted friends is much better than a group of fair-weather acquaintances.

SELF-CARE

Teens have terribly busy days and a lot to balance. In many ways, life is a balancing act and helping your teen prioritize their day is a lifelong gift. Our children are called to go to school, do homework, and find time for family and friends. Most throw in one, or more, time consuming activities such as music, sports, clubs and organizations, or jobs. They tend to have very full days and can let their basic needs suffer. I have three areas I need them to focus on to be better prepared to succeed with all they are called to do. These are sleep, nutrition, and exercise. You will see each one of these can affect the others and good habits can really help your teen with their daily balancing act.

SLEEP

Research shows teens need eight to ten hours of sleep a night. I meet many teens who get substantially less, and it concerns me. We are all better when we are rested. We think more clearly – making fewer mistakes. We retain what we learn throughout the day better when we get sufficient sleep. We are better prepared to compete athletically and handle stressful situations when we are well rested. Growth hormones are released during sleep allowing for better growth and weight can be more stable with good sleep. Sleep often is the first thing a teen will sacrifice as their schedule fills. Our bodies perform best when they go to bed and get up at the same time each day. That is not always possible in the real world, but it should be the goal to strive for as often as possible.

Electronics are often the cause of insufficient teen sleep. They are a huge responsibility to handle at any age, especially younger ages and they are everywhere from the school computer, cell phone, watch, tablet, etc. Electronics are not going away, and we must teach our teens to use them responsibly and in moderation. Whether texting friends, watching video clips, gaming, or scrolling electronics can draw us in and eat up a lot of time, often without us realizing how much time. We owe it to our kids to model responsible use of electronics and help them find their healthy limits. Parental controls for time and content can be a helpful aid, but eventually, your child will leave your watch and need to have self-regulated electronic boundaries. I like to point out to teens that with their current load eight hours of sleep is not always possible, but if they could limit electronic use by twenty minutes a day, five school nights a week they would have 100 extra minutes of sleep a week. That sounds like a goal worth meeting or exceeding.

Good sleep hygiene includes having a wind-down routine. Try to help your teen establish a nightly routine. This can consist of showering or cleansing their face, brushing teeth, and getting into sleepwear. They need to start telling their brain it is getting ready to sleep. Unplug from all electronics ideally sixty minutes before bed, but at least thirty minutes as electronics stimulate the brain and make it hard to fall asleep. Turn down the lights to further reduce brain stimulation and substitute calming activities such as reading, stretching, meditation, journaling, praying, or relaxation exercises. Having a comfortable, peaceful, and uncluttered sleeping space is also helpful. Ask your teen to only use their bed for sleeping so there is a strong mental connection between the bed and sleep. Cut out caffeine in the hours proceeding bedtime. Consider how old and of what quality your teen's mattress or pillow might be and if it needs to be updated. Help them find ways to organize their room and decrease clutter. Ensure the room has good ventilation, cool but comfortable is best for quality sleep. Consider black out curtains to block light and ear plugs or white noise machines to block sounds. If after you implement these techniques, your teen still routinely has trouble falling asleep or staying asleep, then consulting their physician could be helpful to look at medical causes of poor sleep, including anxiety and obstructive sleep apnea.

NUTRITION

It is just so true that we feel better when we eat better. There are many theories on nutrition, but the basics always stay the same. Your body needs lots of vegetables, fruits and proteins and less sugar, fats, and carbs. Understandably your teen is not going to eat perfectly healthy all day every day, but you want them to consider that the habits they start now will likely continue throughout their lives. We are creatures of habit, and it can be hard to change poor eating habits. Even more reason to start healthy habits early. Not all, but many people must work to eat more vegetables. Help your teen explore a variety of vegetables to find new ones to enjoy, get creative with salads and smoothies to incorporate more veggies. Try preparing veggies in new ways. Expand their vegetable horizons. Try to keep your home stocked with a good variety of fresh fruits and vegetables. Seek out and try new recipes with input from your teen. If your teen loses self-control with junk food either do not buy it or buy in small quantities. Help them recognize poor eating habits such as eating when bored or stressed, but not hungry. Even healthy foods can be consumed in abundance. Help them judge portion control. It is true that taste buds develop over time. Encourage retrying foods that they have not liked in the past and retrying them often.

Many teens skip meals-especially breakfast. This is a bad habit for them. Food is fuel for the body, and we do not want to send them out into their day without fuel. Without breakfast they will not feel as energetic or as focused. It will affect their school-work, energy level, and overall mood. Most teens say they either do not have time for breakfast or are not hungry. My reply is breakfast does not have to be a big sit-down meal. Even a little nutrition can go a long way. Brainstorm with your teen what would sound good and be quick. Think grab and go kind of items. Many are willing to drink something even if they do not feel like eating. Explore the idea of smoothies, ideally with added protein, protein bars or shakes. Starting their day with protein can increase focus and give them sustainable energy versus a quick carb boost. Try to mix things up to keep breakfast from getting boring. If they have sports first thing in the morning, ensure a quick breakfast after workout. Brainstorm solutions with your child to ensure they get the nutrition they need to thrive. Consider letting them shop with you and have some input.

EXERCISE

It is recommended that teens get one hour of moderate to high intensity exercise each day. For those not in organized sports, that can take some planning. Only about 25% of our teens achieve this goal. Creating good health habits in the teen years provides better health and self-satisfaction in the short term while instilling habits that can last a lifetime. Exercise benefits heart health, strengthens bones and muscles, enhances sleep, and increases endurance. Exercise releases endorphins that help with stress, anxiety, and depression and helps the brain with better academic performance and memory. In today's world it is easy to develop sedentary habits with more done on-line and more screen-time past times. Meals come ready made and groceries can be delivered via an app. Society is becoming less active.

Help your teen become more active. Role model a physically active lifestyle and invite them to join you. Help them brainstorm a variety of forms of exercise to keep them interested. Suggestions include joining a gym or trying different classes. Think martial arts or self-defense classes to cycling or hot yoga. Be creative and make it fun. Walking can be incredibly beneficial with no class or special equipment required. Encourage adding music but ensure they are aware of their surroundings. Jumping rope, shooting baskets, swimming, biking, exercise videos, dance, hiking, treadmills or ellipticals, and weightlifting are other starter ideas. Be sure to be encouraging and try to tailor to your teens' likes. If they like the outdoors, focus more on outdoor activities versus indoors and if they like to be social, focus on more group activities than solo activities. If your teen has not been active, they are unlikely to go immediately to successfully exercising sixty minutes a day. They will feel like they are a failure and quit. Set a reasonable starting goal of thirty minutes three times a week and build. If they get off track, start again. Celebrate the small victories while reaching for bigger ones. Create a love of movement that will serve them for years to come.

CHAPTER 6:
SOCIAL MEDIA

I t is estimated that at least 95% of teens use social media. One study showed that 22% of tenth-grade girls spend seven or more hours on social media each day. Social media is increasingly linked to depression, and we will discuss more about this aspect when we cover mental health. Earlier when reviewing sleep, we discussed the importance of helping teens regulate electronic usage. For this discussion, we need to talk about safety with social media.

It is a frightening fact that a one-second decision can have lifelong consequences. One moment of indiscretion can haunt for years. College admission boards will freely reveal that when they have two equally matched candidates they need to decide between for admission they will often look at the candidates' social media. What they see can be the deciding factor when competition is high. I have heard similar explanations from coaches at all levels, and in job interviews. Your teen needs to think about each post. If they snap and post a picture at a party where they are looking great, having a fun moment, making good choices, dancing with friends and it shows others drinking in the background it can still reflect negatively on them. They must consider every aspect of the photo carefully. It is a huge responsibility at an immature age. Encourage them to think, is this something I could proudly show my grandparents? If you would not show grandma and grandpa, it might not be a good post.

Another consideration with an on-line presence is what they write or how they respond. The grandparent rule can work well here also. If it is not informative, funny in an unharmful way, kind, supportive, or uplifting, do not hit send. All too often replies are made that are unkind or downright mean as filters are lost responding to a post versus saying something to someone in person. There is no problem having a differing opinion from a post. If so compelled, your teen might post a thoughtful reply expressing an alternative point of view, but they need to show respect to differing opinions and stop replying if the exchange is not a productive one.

Our kids must be told young and often reminded that criminals keep getting smarter. They can NEVER give out personal information in public or with someone just known through social media. If they make a friend gaming or chatting they really cannot know if that person is a sixteen-year-old remarkably similar to them or a sixty-year-old with a criminal record. So much caution is required with the huge responsibility of social media. If in doubt – DON'T!

Social media can be positive. Studies suggest less evidence of depression with social media use when it is active use. This means they are not just passively scrolling but commenting and posting themselves. Social media can allow for sharing ideas and educational experiences that provide a positive connection. Teens who handle social media well communicate with their parents about technology use and have parents who role model limiting their social media use.

CHAPTER 7:
MENTAL HEALTH

It is increasingly stressful to be a teen. Teens are trying to figure out who they are and where they fit into the world. They are pulled in many different directions. Sports and fine arts compete at increasingly higher levels, college-level classes are being completed in high school, good grades and high standardized test scores are expected, they need more extracurriculars to look competitive for colleges, special programs, or jobs. Some may feel discriminated against or poorly understood and sadly some do not feel safe due to bullying or social contacts. Teens are balancing increasingly more and more at an age where their brain is still trying to develop. We must recognize their stress and help them find ways to process it. Strong mental health has always been important, but the importance and need grows with each passing year. As the cases needing care increase steadily, resources struggle to meet the demand. Being proactive and not waiting for a crisis is paramount. The earlier treatment is started the better the results and it can help prevent more severe and lasting problems in the future. The goal is to develop skills that serve them into adulthood. Seeking help is not a weakness but a way to better oneself and become stronger. If the stress controls them despite best efforts, then it is time to get additional help. Resources for additional support include the school counselor, pediatrician, licensed therapist, psychologist, or psychiatrist.

Ask your teen how they handle stress. There is a strong chance they will say they do not know, but hopefully they can list one or two things they have found that help them cope. It is helpful to brainstorm additional ways to handle stress. Suggestions include:

- **Deep breathing** – This can be done anywhere and is backed by scientific proof showing the beneficial activation of the parasympathetic nervous system. This will lower the blood pressure, slow the heart rate, and calm the brain. Try a 4-second inhale, 4-second breath hold and 4-second exhale, repeating at least three times.

- **Journaling** – allows for quiet reflection and can help clarify thoughts.

- **Talking it out** – This can be with parents, friends, or a trusted adult. It can help clarify thoughts and hopefully lead to feeling understood while gaining a new perspective or helpful idea.

- **Exercise** – not only do you get the physical benefit, you also release endorphins. Endorphins can reduce stress and improve mood.

- **Warm baths or showers** – can help relax the body to release stress.

- **Praying** – for the faith-filled, turning your problems and stresses over to a God that can handle your stress and already has a plan for the stress can be a huge help.

- **Using your creative side** – whether it is drawing, listening to music, or playing music all can help let go of stress.

- **Pets** – petting or cuddling a pet can be an effective way to relax for many.

- **Relaxation apps** – can lead to a good process of self-relaxation skills.

- **Acts of service** – we cannot help but feel better when we do something nice for someone else. Even something small and seemingly insignificant like giving a smile, kind word, or helping hand can lift a day.

There is no one right way to relieve stress, but knowing what works well for your teen and having a go-to list of stress relievers thought out beforehand is powerful. Many studies show the escalation of anxiety and depression increasing steadily with the increase in social media use. Reasons for this increase can include:

- Comparing oneself to a filtered and photoshopped image

- Seeing a post of people that seem to have it all together with a perfectly happy life and feelings of falling short

- Sleep deprivation or poor sleep resulting from too much time on social media

- Unkind comments to a post or not getting as many likes on posts as others

There are even bullying types that will take an unflattering photo and post it for others to see and often make fun of. Social media greatly contributes to the rising number of anxiety and depression diagnoses. Following the cautions discussed under social media with your teen, limiting their time on social media, and discussing what is real, meaningful, and worthy of their thoughts and attention can help.

CHAPTER 8:

DRUGS

Buckle your seatbelts! There is a lot to cover under drugs, which is critical to your child's safety and well-being. This is an area where parents need to stay updated on current trends nationwide and locally. Information is needed and powerful. A good conversation often starts with asking your teen what they see at school—about their experiences and what they know about the various drugs. An exchange of information and back-and-forth dialogue proves more productive than a "drugs are bad" lecture. This list is not all inclusive and ever-changing, but here is some need-to-know information:

OVER-THE-COUNTER

Encourage your teen to let you know everything they are taking. Over-the-counter medications must be used for the right reasons, in the proper doses, and proper combinations. You need to be involved in what they are taking and accessing if it works. Teens are not known for being very consistent with medications, so if their allergies are horrible and medication is not helping, are they taking it daily? If they are taking ibuprofen for a headache and it helps-how often are they getting those headaches and taking medication? They are on the bridge from childhood to adulthood, but still need oversight. It pays to be involved. Many teens believe supplements to be harmless, but they do require a certain amount of caution. Creatine is popular among weightlifters and increasingly added to supplements. The total amount must be considered and kept within safety guidelines. Many supplements and energy drinks contain caffeine. When used in excess or combination with other substances caffeine can lead to cardiac complications including an irregular heart rate, heart attacks or death. Dry scooping, taking prework out with minimal or no water, is a current trend that has led to hospitalization of several teens trying to elevate their work outs. It was popularized on Tic-Tok videos. This trend will be replaced with a new and possibly even more dangerous one. Parents must keep watch with open lines of communication to keep their teens safe.

MARIJUANA

Many states have legalized marijuana, which can send teens a confusing message that marijuana is safe. The effects of marijuana on a young and developing brain are quite different than the effects on a developed brain. Brains complete their development around the age of twenty-two-years-old. Marijuana can affect normal brain development causing learning and memory problems, coordination difficulties, poor judgment, and slow reaction times. The younger marijuana use begins the more addictive and likely to lead to lifelong addiction problems.

In my years of practice, I have seen marijuana destroy the lives of some amazing teens and their families. Teens often want a job to earn additional income, which can be a great leap toward maturity, but it can also introduce them to other entry-level employees. Frequently those addicted to marijuana or other drugs share the same job position as teens due to inconsistency in their work and ability to maintain employment. One police officer shared he has seen more teens get introduced to drugs at job sites then from peers of the same age. I can think of one very bright sixteen-year-old who decided to try marijuana offered by a co-worker after a work shift. In his mind, he was trying it; what could be the harm in trying it once? For him, it was the end of his goals and dreams. From the first try he was addicted! Marijuana took over his life. It made it difficult to finish high school and impossible to consider higher education. He has been arrested and sent to multiple rehabilitation programs with no lasting effect. Over eight years later he continues to work menial jobs to pay rent and get more marijuana. He rarely has decent groceries. The love and support of his family, exhaustive efforts with therapy and judicial system repercussions have not been enough to break his addiction. He should be a college graduate with a successful job and bright future, but his decision to try marijuana took that future away from him. Unfortunately, this scenario is all too common. Our teens must know the dangers of drugs and that even just trying something once can end or significantly alter their lives.

VAPING

Vaping has become so common that you rarely hear cigarettes mentioned any more. Obviously, cigarettes did not get any healthier. They remain addictive with multiple risks to health including cancer, respiratory, and cardiac disease. Vaping has become much more prevalent partly because of flavors, partly due to a false notion that vaping is less dangerous than cigarettes, and partly because of higher levels of nicotine. One vape pod can have the nicotine equivalent to an entire pack of cigarettes. These high nicotine levels make vaping extremely addictive. Young brains still developing are at increased risk of addiction compared to fully developed brains. Dangers of vaping, beyond addiction, include lung damage, carcinogen exposure, increased likelihood of using other drugs, decreased attention span and decreased athletic performance.

I see many teens that try vaping and other drugs to help with their stress or anxiety. Unfortunately, these substances only increase their overall stress and anxiety levels. Once again, the importance of frequent discussion for both mental health and the dangers of drugs is so important. We want to be there as parents to help and guide them, so they do not feel the need to turn to drugs to try and solve their problems.

ALCOHOL

Alcohol is a powerful and addictive drug that can lead to impairment such as diminished reaction times, decreased coordination, impaired vision, and problems exercising good judgment. In high enough doses it leads to death. Once again, the younger the exposure to alcohol the more likely it is to end up with brain damage and addiction. Teens who start drinking at fifteen are five times more likely to develop an alcohol addiction than those who wait till age twenty-one. Binge drinking is the most harmful form of drinking, it is drinking four drinks for females or five drinks for males in two hours and is popular among teens—teen drinking and driving results in about 4,000 teen deaths a year and multiple more injuries.

Teens often feel the need to drink to fit in, but statistically 30% of teens aged fifteen to seventeen have drunk alcohol in the last month. So, while it is common 70% are not drinking-everyone is not "doing it". It is OK to say "NO." Teen drinking is illegal, it reduces the chance of graduating high school, and increases the risk of assault and rape.

Many adults enjoy the taste of alcoholic drinks. When consumed responsibly, there might be some cardiac benefits. If adults drink, they must model responsible partying by drinking in small to moderate amounts and not driving when impaired. Your teen is watching you and is likely to copy you. Setting a good example is crucial.

NARCOTICS

At the time of writing, we are in a fentanyl crisis. Fentanyl is a synthetic opioid that is much stronger than other opioids. More teens are dying of drug overdoses than car accidents. The conniving of the criminal element trying to get our kids addicted to drugs is staggering. There is an exceptionally fine line between the amount of fentanyl that kills versus the amount that becomes an addiction from the first use. They will lace what appears to be normal candy and everyday medications with fentanyl to get an unexpecting consumer addicted. We truly must always be on guard and question everything. Gone are the days of our kids sharing candy or over-the-counter medication with friends, unless they can be 100% certain where that candy or medication came from. We must err on the side of caution as the consequence of making a poor judgment can be addiction or death. This sounds dramatic, but this is the current reality. Narcan reverses the effect of opioids and is now available over-the-counter as a nasal spray to be administered with expected drug overdoses. Having Narcan readily available can be lifesaving.

I talk to my kids frequently about the danger of drugs and the ever-growing criminal element. They are aware, but still at risk-as this example illustrates. My son loves to work out. He is curious about different supplements, and we have frequent conversations about what I feel is safe and what concerns me for him to use. He gets a lot of advice from friends and YouTube videos, and we evaluate together the advice for merit. I am fortunate that he seeks, respects, and values my input. Recently he was working out with a friend and took a supplement from his friend. When I picked him up from the gym, he told me what he had taken. I expressed my concern over that choice. He saw an error and said to me that he was sorry, he knows he is supposed to clear all supplements with me first. I told him that while that is true and I want to approve of what he takes, I had a much greater concern. I explained that we really do not know where that pill came from and that it was not tainted. He responded that it came from a good and trusted friend. I agreed that it did come from a friend I trust would not **knowingly** give him anything tainted with drugs, but that we do not know where the friend obtained the supplement. I reminded him that in the world he is growing up in today, we must be extra cautious and that his choice really scared me. It was a good and fresh reminder to be constantly vigilant. He saw just how easy it could be to get exposed to an addictive drug and gave me permission to tell his story in hopes of helping others.

Caution must be exercised anytime your child is prescribed pain medications. Avoiding or minimal use of opioids should be the norm. Common prescription opioids include codeine, hydrocodone (Vicodin), Oxycodone (OxyContin or Percocet), morphine, and fentanyl. Make sure if your child is experiencing surgery or chronic pain that you are working with your doctor to maximize all areas of pain control with minimal or no opioid use. Many have started their addiction with prescribed medication used as directed. The medical community is working to revise pain control to make it safer and more effective. Be an active part of your child's pain management team and ensure they use a multimodal approach to pain management. Discard all prescription opioid medications once they are no longer needed. Whether prescribed for you or your child, turn in leftover medication to a secure return facility and do not have them in your home.

PREPARE YOUR TEEN TO SAY NO!

As it is incredibly likely that your teen will be in a situation where they are offered a drug, help them know how to say no. It is even a good idea to role-play a few suggestions so they feel more comfortable using them. You can brainstorm a response that works for your child, here are some starter ideas:

- NO – plain, effective and to the point – no explanation required.

- I've quit – this suggestion was told to me by a wise teen years ago. It works even if they never started using drugs and does not invite much room for discussion.

- My parents/coaches drug test me – You can Amazon drug tests or pick them up at a pharmacy and have them readily available for home use. Whether it is your choice to screen your teen or not they can certainly use you as a reason to avoid drug exposure.

- I have a competition coming up – will need to be in top shape to compete.

THE X PLAN

Another way to help your teen avoid drugs is to have a preset plan to help them leave an event if they feel uncomfortable for any reason. The idea is that you have a preset text (like the letter X or a specific emoji) they can send to you or other trusted drivers. When you see they have sent you the agreed-upon text, you call them and tell them there is a family emergency and you need to pick them up. The thought is they send a discreet, quick text that does not draw attention like a long typed-out text, and then you provide their way out. This works best with a no-questions-asked promise. They share with you only what they want to share and when they want. Knowing they can get a safe ride without being questioned makes them much more likely to use the plan. I first heard this plan explained by a reformed drug addict. They stated they started using drugs when they were in a situation where they did not see a way to say no or to get out. From that experience, their addiction grew. They felt if they could have had a plan to get out of potentially dangerous situations, it could have prevented many years of pain.

Several years ago, one of my kids called me at 3:00 a.m. and asked me to pick him up from a friend's house. I was shocked with so many questions, but just jumped in the car to get him. On the ride home, he stayed quiet and then started sharing. What he shared led to lifesaving actions for some of his friends. He made a tough choice at a young age. His friends got in trouble and were angry, but they were alive. My child certainly gets the credit for his actions, but I like to think that the discussions we had leading up to that night along with an I'll come and get you anytime with no questions asked guarantee from me helped with his choice that night.

CHAPTER 9:
SEX

Teens can get a lot of unsolicited sexual attention from peers and adults, even trusted adults. This could be in the form of crude jokes, comments, looks or touching. It can be hard to know how to handle this new attention. Talk to them about boundaries and encourage them to speak up if someone makes them uncomfortable. If you have examples from your past of how you have handled unwanted attention, share your examples with them. If you handled it well, they could learn from you or tell them you wish you would have handled it differently. Personalize the discussion to make it more relevant and meaningful. Role-play can also be helpful here to empower them to handle what might come their way.

Beyond the birds and the bees discussion, you need to have the emotional discussion. Sex is a big deal! It needs to be when your child is emotionally ready and fully prepared. 30% to 35% of teens are sexually active. Of course, this means 65-70% are not having sex. If your teen plans to wait, help them plan how to say no so they are clearly understood. Encourage them to avoid situations likely to lead to sex such as impaired thinking from alcohol or drugs or being alone, one-on-one, and unsupervised. Encourage like-minded friend groups.

Ask your teen, or beyond teen years child, to talk to you when they are considering having sex and before their first sexual encounter. Let them know you want to ensure they are ready for such a big step. If they are mature enough to consider sex, they should be mature enough to discuss their choice with a caring adult. As having sex is a big deal, it is best as a thought-out and planned activity and not an impulsive one with little or no preparation. Ensure your child is not pressured and discuss how they will feel if their partner leaves them afterward or tells others. Ask how they think having sex will affect their relationship with the partner. Remind them that it is possible to get pregnant the first time even when on birth control and using protection. Are they ready to accept the possibility of a pregnancy? Remind them of the risk of sexually transmitted diseases (STDs) and the importance of using a condom even with other sources of birth control. Consider starting females on birth control, buying condoms to have readily available, and getting vaccinated to protect against Human Papilloma Virus (HPV). HPV is a sexually transmitted virus carried by 90% of the adult population that can cause various cancers. Approximately 50% of people get HPV on their first sexual encounter. The vaccine protects against the most common strains of HPV. Remain approachable and not judgmental or emotional–yours is the voice of reason when your teen might think more with their heart or hormones.

CHAPTER 10:
ADVOCATION

As your teen matures, they must learn to speak up and advocate for themselves and others. Hopefully, you have already set a good example of effectively advocating for them in the past and they can grow from the foundation you started. First have your teen make sure that what they are advocating for is important. Many causes can be advocated for, but make sure they are using their energies on what really matters to them. As the teen years can come with a lot of drama, my general advice is to be active when a matter affects you or someone who cannot stand up for themselves, but not to assert oneself in every peer conflict. Once they have identified a situation they feel needs to be addressed then they need to speak calmly, politely, and intelligently. They need to listen to opposing opinions and consider all sides. Ultimately, they may need to learn to disagree.

The middle school and high school years are great for growing independence in their schoolwork. They must learn to ask for help when needed. Teachers are not mind readers, but most will bend over backward to help a teen they know is sincerely trying. Usually, the teen must make the first move by asking a clarifying question, seeking additional explanation, or tutoring times. Talking to teachers and other adults in authority can be scary for many teens. Coach them up and let them practice with you. If they are too shy to speak up in person, emailing a teacher could be a good start. Build on each experience and learn what works well for them. These skills will serve them well lifelong. It is not appropriate for you to keep fighting their fights for them. Make them strong advocates for themselves.

CHAPTER 11:
FAITH

For many, faith defines who they are and what they do. It pushes them to be a better person. If you are a parent of faith, pray for your child, pray for their friends, teachers, choices, health, driving, and future. Pray for big and little things. Pray before speaking with them to have the words they need to hear, which will reach them. Pray to hear them and understand them. Pray to find what is best for them as a unique individual and not just what you think is best for them. Pray! Pray! Pray!

Share your faith with your child. Their faith journey may look a little different than yours, which is OK. Let them know what you believe and why. Ask them what they believe and why. Demonstrate to them how faith can help guide them and help relieve the stresses of being a teen. Try to pray together and ask them if there is anything specific they would like you to pray about for them or pray about together. Share examples of how your faith has helped you in times of need or inspired you to reach new goals.

Personally, I know there is so much I cannot control and believing that God is ever present and able to handle whatever life brings is a huge help. I think of a prisoner of war hero I met who was injured and held in an empty, dark stone cell with one small "meal" a day and other abusive conditions. She really had nothing but her faith, and with that she had everything! She survived and thrived after such a horrific ordeal. I tell myself and my kids that no matter what circumstances you find yourself in, you always have your faith and the power of prayer. I find it comforting.

CHAPTER 12:
CONCLUSION

I hope a few of the ideas in these pages have inspired you. Hopefully, there was a new idea or a reminder of something you already knew, that resonated with you as something that could strengthen your relationship with your teen. Relationships are formed over time, and the best ones are grown intentionally with love and dedication. Clearly, you love your teen, or you would not be reading this book. Ideally, you feel your love returned, but often teens are not demonstrative and take parents for granted. Be the consistency and strength they need. Let them know you believe in them so they can find the confidence to believe in themselves. Use your words, actions, and time with them to build them up. Be cautious with criticism and make sure it is productive. Get support from others and learn from others. Set healthy limits and boundaries that are clear and reinforce them. Teenagers need this support!

Now that you have finished the parent part of this book it is time to ask your teen to read their part. While the parent part was kept fairly short the teen part is even shorter hoping to make it more feasible to get their participation. I would introduce the book as something you chose to aid you in being the best parent you can be, and as relationships are best when both are working well together or on the same page you need their participation. Ask them to read their small part to help meet your efforts. Maybe offer an incentive for finishing it in a week.

CHAPTER 13:

PARENTAL DISCUSSION OR REFLECTION QUESTIONS

1. What did you read that resonated the most with you?

2. What area of parenting do you struggle with the most?

3. What are three things that the book has encouraged you to do to supplement your parenting techniques?

4. What two habits would you like to break or change to be a more effective parent?

5. How can you be more approachable to your teen?

6. List three things you can do to support your teen better.

BIBLIOGRAPHY

"American Heart Association Recommendations for Physical Activity in Adults and Kids." *Www.Heart.Org*, 28 July 2022, www.heart.org/en/healthy-living/fitness/fitness-basics/aha-recs-for-physical-activity-in-adults.

Chapman, Gary. "Learn More about Yourself." *Learn More About Yourself*, 5lovelanguages.com/quizzes/.

"Get the Facts about Underage Drinking." *National Institute on Alcohol Abuse and Alcoholism*, U.S. Department of Health and Human Services, www.niaaa.nih.gov/publications/brochures-and-fact-sheets/underage-drinking.

Hyder, Eileen, and Lucinda Becker. "How to make your social media communication inclusive." *Inclusive Communication*, 2022, https://doi.org/10.4135/9781071901205.

New, Michael J. *The Corner: New CDC Data Shows Continued Decline in Teen Sexual Activity*. Owlkids Books, 2023.

Suni, Eric, and Alex Dimitriu. *National Sleep Foundation Pamphlets*. National Sleep Foundation.

"Tween and Teen Health Tween and Teen Health." *Mayo Clinic*, Mayo Foundation for Medical Education and Research, 23 Aug. 2023, www.mayoclinic.org/healthy-lifestyle/tween-and-teen-health/basics/tween-and-teen-health/hlv-20049436.

"Underage Drinking." *Centers for Disease Control and Prevention*, Centers for Disease Control and Prevention, 26 Oct. 2022, www.cdc.gov/alcohol/fact-sheets/underage-drinking.htm.